Wales Coast Path: The Snowdonia Coast

Text: *Sioned Bannister*

Series editor: *Tony Bowerman*

Photographs: *Sioned Bannister, Ian Warburton, Carl Rogers, Shutterstock, The National Library of Wales, © Crown copyright (2012) Visit Wales*

Design: *Carl Rogers*

Northern Eye Books

ISBN 978-1-908632-85-2

A CIP catalogue record for this book is available from the British Library

Printed in the UK

Cover: *Harlech Castle (Walk 4)*

Important Advice: The routes described in this book are undertaken at the reader's own risk. Walkers should take into account their level of fitness, wear suitable footwear and clothing, and carry food and water. It is also advisable to take the relevant OS map with you in case you get lost and leave the area covered by our maps.

Whilst every care has been taken to ensure the accuracy of the route directions, the publishers cannot accept responsibility for errors or omissions, or for changes in the details given. Nor can the publisher and copyright owners accept responsibility for any consequences arising from the use of this book.

If you find any inaccuracies in either the text or maps, please either write to us or email us at the addresses below. Thank you.

First published in 2012. This revised edition published in 2019 by:

Northern Eye Books Limited
Northern Eye Books, Tattenhall, Cheshire CH3 9PX

Email: tony@northerneyebooks.com

For sales enquiries, please call 01928 723 744

www.walescoastpath.co.uk
www.northerneyebooks.co.uk

Instagram: @wales_coast_path
@northerneyebooks

Twitter: @WalesCoastUK
@northerneyeboo

Contents

The **Wales Coast Path**

Wales is the only country in the world with a path around its entire coast. The long-distance **Wales Coast Path** offers 870 miles/1440 kilometres of unbroken coastal walking, from the outskirts of the walled city of Chester in the north to the market town of Chepstow in the south.

There's something new around every corner. Visually stunning and rich in both history and wildlife, the path promises ever-changing views, wildflowers and seabirds, as well as castles, coves and coastal pubs. In fact, the Wales Coast Path runs through 1 Marine Nature Reserve, 2 National Parks, 3 Areas of Outstanding Natural Beauty, 11 National Nature Reserves, 14 Heritage Coasts, and 23 Historic Landscapes. And, to cap it all, the **Wales Coast Path** links up with the long-distance Offa's Dyke path at either end: creating a complete, 1,030 mile circuit of the whole of Wales.

The Mawddach estuary and Cadair Idris from Barmouth Panorama viewpoint

The Snowdonia Coast

Cardigan Bay embraces the dramatic sweep of the Welsh coastline, from Bardsey island on the tip of Llŷn, in the north, to Strumble Head in Pembrokeshire, in the south. It takes in parts of two National Parks: Snowdonia and Pembrokeshire, and three different counties: Gwynedd, Ceredigion and Pembrokeshire.

The striking northern section between Porthmadog and Aberystwyth is as varied as it is beautiful. Characterised by vast beaches and rugged cliffs, the coast offers superb walking with ever-changing views and a wealth of wildlife.

"Wales is one of the most picturesque countries in the world, in which Nature displays herself in her wildest, boldest, and loveliest forms…" George Borrow, *Wild Wales*, 1862

TOP 10 **Walks:** The Snowdonia Coast

THESE TEN CAREFULLY CHOSEN WALKS will take you to some of the loveliest places on the northern part of Cardigan Bay, on the **Wales Coast Path**. Each easy-to-follow, circular walk includes a stunning stretch of the coast path and a visit to a special place. Along the way you'll enjoy harbours and bays, exhilarating clifftops and vast open beaches. Visit ancient stones, a mighty castle and a fantasy village; watch for seabirds, seals and dolphins. These are walks to remember.

Porthmadog & Moel y Gest page 8

Portmeirion page 14

Ynys Llanfihangel-y-Traethau page 20

Harlech Beach & Llanfair Cliffs page 26

Yachts moored in Porthmadog harbour

Porthmadog & Moel-y-Gest

A moderate walk to the summit of a small hill overlooking the town of Porthmadog

What to expect:
Good footpaths, quiet lanes and a short town trail

Distance/time: 7km / 4½ miles. Allow 3 hours

Start: Pay and Display car park in Porthmadog (from the southern end of the High Street, turn into Madog Street then, turn right)

Grid ref: SH 570 387

Ordnance Survey Map: OS Explorer OL 18 Snowdonia *Harlech, Porthmadog & Y Bala*

After the walk: Cafés, restaurants and pubs in Porthmadog

Walk outline

This lovely walk first leads to the top of Moel-y-Gest, a small hill overlooking Porthmadog. On a clear day there are stunning views: to the right the Llŷn Peninsula's long arm sweeps out into the Irish Sea, while to the south, the mountainous layers of Cardigan Bay stretch out as far as St David's Head. The walk descends the far side of the hill into the pretty village of Borth-y-Gest before following a historic wharf back to the town centre.

Porthmadog

Before William Alexander Madocks built the cob in 1811, the land around Porthmadog was open marsh that was often flooded by the sea. Madocks' created dry land and built Porthmadog upon it—the town that bears his name. By 1825, a harbour and wharf had risen on the new land, and fifteen years later the High Street was begun.

The town grew rapidly around the slate mining industry of the Ffestiniog Valleys. Britain's expanding industrial cities needed roofing and the local mountains yielded a fortune in roofing slates. Slates were carted from the quarries to the harbour at Porthmadog and shipped around the world.

Harbour café

Pied flycatcher

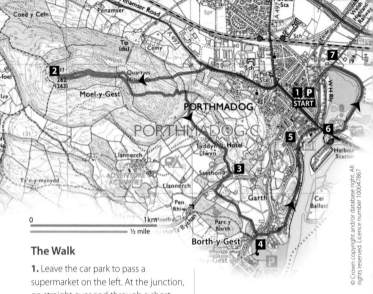

The Walk

1. Leave the car park to pass a supermarket on the left. At the junction, go straight over and through a short alleyway to the **High Street**. Turn right and follow the High Street. Go straight over the crossroads then cross the road at the next pedestrian crossing.

Continue until you reach the roundabout, then turn left to walk along **Penamser Road**. Walk on past **St John's Church**.

St John's was built in 1873. The ashes of R.S. Thomas, the renowned Welsh poet, are buried in the graveyard.

Soon after a camping shop on the right, you'll reach a lay-by on the left. Take the footpath in the far corner, leading up through the trees. Soon, at a junction go straight ahead and over a stile.

Follow the path to the left and up a steep bank. At the top junction, bear right. Continue ahead and follow a steep rocky path to emerge at the summit of **Moel-y-Gest**.

Moel-y-Gest translates literally as 'Gest's Mountain', but at only 263 metres high it's more of a hill. Slate was once quarried from its slopes.

2. Continue, to cross the second, slightly higher summit, then return to the first, lower top. Re-trace your steps to the junction at the top of the steep bank and turn right here. Cross a couple of stiles to emerge at a caravan park, walk past the rear of the hotel and head along the tarmac drive.

Coastal walking: *A Wales Coast Path fingerpost points towards Borth-y-Gest*

3. At the main road, cross and then turn right along the pavement to pass the speed-restriction signs. Take the next left turning into a lay-by, and walk beside a stone wall to pass a driveway, then turn left onto a rough track.

Follow the track through a gate beside a cottage and continue along the path, which soon leads into a small field.

To the right here is **Parc y Borth***, a 15-hectare Nature Reserve made up of ancient oak woodland and wildflower meadows. In summer, look out for woodpeckers and pied flycatchers.*

Cross the field and go through the gate at the far end. Follow the short path, then head between the houses to emerge by the bay in **Borth-y-Gest**.

Borth-y-Gest is much older than Porthmadog; there is thought to have been a settlement here since the 12th century. However, it too grew up around the shipping industry and the village was once famed for its shipbuilding yards.

Porthmadog harbour: *Sailing boats moored alongside Porthmadog Yacht Club*

4. Cross the road, then take the path to the left alongside a stone wall and up the steps. At the top, keep ahead and then, as the road bends to the left, continue ahead to follow a public footpath sign along a tarmac path that leads downhill to the **wharf road**.

The wharf was once the hub of Porthmadog. Majestic schooners, brigs and barquentines would line the quayside awaiting their slate cargoes or off-loading ballast. Further along lies Oakeley Wharf, named after one of the wealthiest local, slate quarry owners.

Continue along the wharf road, passing boat yards and flats on the right. You'll emerge at the harbour after passing the **yacht club** on the right.

5. Continue past a small green on the right. Near the top of the **slipway**, bear right to walk across a pedestrian area with benches. Aim for the top right corner and walk through a narrow passage. Continue ahead, past the community centre and **tourist information centre** on the left.

6. At the main road, cross over and turn right. Just before the record shop, turn left to find a track and gate. Go through the gate and follow the track across the

sluice gates and then onto a wider path around a curved embankment.

This embankment is known as **Cob Crwn**, *or 'Round Cob', and provides an outlet for flood water from the harbour.*

7. When the path meets a road, turn left. Pass an old mill on the right, then cross the railway line and take the next left into the car park to complete the walk. ♦

Porthmadog shipbuilders
Porthmadog ships were some of the finest in the world and during the 19th century the harbour was lined with shipbuilders' yards. But when slate exports declined, the shipbuilders developed the 'Western Ocean Yachts', designed for the salt-cod trade of Newfoundland. These beautiful two- and three-masted schooners were sturdy enough to cross wild oceans yet small enough to navigate the rocky shores and narrow estuaries of the New World.

Portmeirion village fountain and square

Portmeirion

An easy walk exploring the beautiful surroundings of Portmeirion

What to expect:
Good footpaths, cycle route, quiet lanes and the village of Portmeirion

Distance/time: 8km / 5 miles. Allow 3 hours (longer for a visit to the village)

Start: Pay and Display car park in Porthmadog (from the southern end of the High Street, turn into Madog Street then turn right)

Grid ref: SH 570 387

Ordnance Survey Map: OS Explorer OL 18 Snowdonia *Harlech, Porthmadog & Y Bala*

After the walk: Cafés, restaurants and pubs in Porthmadog or in Portmeirion (if you're visiting the village)

Walk outline

A pretty walk that leaves the town of Porthmadog by the famous Cob embankment, from where there are spectacular views across the estuary and to the mountains Snowdonia. The route then heads up into farmland behind Portmeirion village before dropping down to it, with the chance to explore. The return journey is made through a quiet village and back along the Cob.

Portmeirion

Precariously balanced on the coast, Portmeirion is an Italianate village set amidst subtropical gardens that has been attracting tourists, artists, and the media for years. This bizarre but beautiful place is the work of the eccentric Welsh architect Clough Williams-Ellis. He bought the crumbling estate at the end of the First World War and set about transforming it into a utopian fantasy. It became his life's work and between 1925 and 1975 he laboured tirelessly on designing, building and renovating the village.

Today, Portmeirion is run as a tourist attraction and includes a hotel, apartments, restaurant, cafés and shops.

Ffestiniog railway

Colourful colonnade

The Walk

1. Leave the car park to pass a supermarket on the left. At the junction, turn left, then very soon left again at the next junction by the petrol station. Cross the railway and walk over the bridge. Cross the road by the record shop and head for the **Ffestiniog Railway** platform.

The Ffestiniog Railway is the world's oldest independent railway company, established in 1832. Its original purpose was to transport slate from the Ffestiniog mines to the harbour at Porthmadog.

2. Keep ahead and follow the railway line away from the station. Follow the line along the top of the embankment called **The Cob** for almost a mile.

The Cob ('Y Cob) is a sea wall built in 1811 by William Alexander Madocks. Its construction meant that acres of land were reclaimed from the sea, on which Madocks built Porthmadog and Tremadog.

Just before **Boston Lodge sidings**, take the steep steps down to the road and cross carefully. Go down the steps/ramp and onto the path. Turn right, passing an old **toll house**.

3. Soon after a lay-by, cross the road and bear right at a bridleway sign, up a track.

Turn left at the top and very soon bear right to cross the railway. Follow the footpath sign through a gate for a stony path uphill. At a fork keep left to reach a metal gate.

Go through the gate and stay ahead to eventually reach another gate at a cross-road of bridleways.

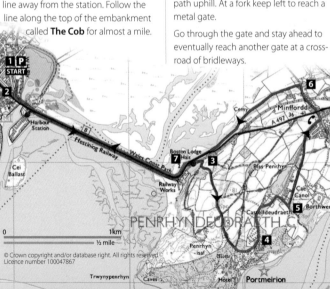

© Crown copyright and/or database right. All rights reserved. Licence number 100047867

Smoke between clouds: *A Ffestioniog Railway steam train crossing the Cob*

The farm to the right is called **Penrhyn Isaf** *and in 1812 was the scene of a brutal murder. A man known as Hwntw Mawr (or the 'Giant Southerner') was working on repairs to the Cob when he crept up to the farmhouse, hoping to steal money and valuables. However, he bumped into a maid, Mary Jones, whom he fatally stabbed in a panic. He was eventually captured, charged with murder, and publicly hanged in Dolgellau. It was one of the last hangings in the county.*

Go straight across and follow a path alongside a stone wall on the left. It will descend to a larger stone wall, so go through the gap and gate and keep ahead to another large wall and pass through the gap/gate.

The path now winds along the edge of a fence, to your right. When you reach a wooden gate don't go through it; instead, turn right, between staggered posts, and follow the path to the car park. (To visit **Portmeirion village**, follow the signs. Charges apply. Dogs are not permitted).

Watery panorama: *Looking back across the Cob and the tidal saltmarsh of Traeth Mawr*

Please don't miss the unique, fairytale village of Portmeirion. The surrounding land, known as The Gwyllt (or 'The Wilderness'), is a delight, too, and full of rare and tropical plants. Don't miss the Dog Cemetery or the idyllic beach, either.

4. Continue ahead to follow the exit signs, bearing left out of the car park, then left along the exit drive.

Continue past tennis courts and **Castell Deudraeth**. Just beyond a Give Way sign, turn right through the parking area, and then right again, down the lane.

5. At a yellow, arched seat, turn left and follow the track to its end (keep straight ahead at a bridleway sign beside a cottage and again at the next).

The track soon becomes a tarmaced lane. Continue along the lane, and turn left at the junction to reach the main road. Cross the road to another narrow lane, which runs between the end of a terrace and a detached house. Follow the lane downhill.

6. Cross the **railway line** and, at the bottom of the hill, turn left along a wider lane. Follow this to meet the main road at a T-junction, then bear right along the pavement towards **Boston Lodge**.

Boston Lodge is so named because William Madocks was MP for Boston, Lincolnshire.

7. At the end of the lay-by, bear right for the footpath and cycleway. Go under the wooden arch, past the **Toll House**.

8. Follow the base of the Cob back to **Porthmadog**. Retrace your steps to the car park to complete the walk. ♦

Portmeirion Pottery

The Portmeirion Pottery *brand is almost as celebrated as the village itself. It began when Clough Williams-Ellis asked his daughter Susan to create a range of pottery for the Portmeirion gift shop. The pottery was a huge success and Susan went on to become one of the world's most respected pottery designers. Her best known design is the instantly recognisable Botanic range. Launched in 1972, it still sells well around the world today.*

Walking along the Ynys shoreline

Ynys Llanfihangel-y-Traethau

A short, easy walk with stunning views and a pretty church to explore

What to expect:
Good footpaths and a small section over the marshy estuary flats

Distance/time: 3km / 2 miles. Allow 1½ hours

Start: Car park at Ynys (From Talsarnau, follow the A496 south, turning right for Harlech. Go over the railway then as road bends sharp left turn first right and follow the lane

Grid ref: SH 599 357

Ordnance Survey Map: OS Explorer OL 18 Snowdonia *Harlech, Porthmadog & Y Bala*

After the walk: Cafés, restaurants and pubs in Harlech or Talsarnau

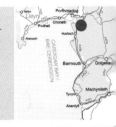

Walk outline

This easy but fabulous walk explores a hidden gem on the Cardigan Bay coast. Ynys Llanfihangel-y-Traethau is the full name of this tiny waterside hamlet, but it's often known by the shorter Ynys (meaning 'island'). The walk first leads along a tidal estuary, before heading across low farmlands above the river. The walk offers stunning views of the Dwyryd Estuary and there's the chance to explore a charming church.

Ynys

Ynys (meaning 'island' in Welsh) was a real island for many centuries until an embankment built at the start of the 19th century linked it to the mainland (close to what is now the main road to Harlech).

Distant Portmeirion

Once a busy shipping port, Ynys was also the lowest point at which travellers could cross the Dwyryd Estuary to Borth-y-Gest and Porthmadog. Crossings were treacherous because of the tides, strong currents and quicksands. Pont Briwet (Briwet Bridge) was built in 1860, but the Grade II listed structure that has crossed the river for over 150 years will soon be demolished and replaced by a new road and rail bridge.

Grey heron

WARNING: This walk is best undertaken at low tide and should not be attempted if the tide is coming in. Check tide times before setting off.

The Walk

1. Face the estuary and turn left to walk along the road, passing a house named '**Glan Meirion**'.

There was once a busy quayside here as it was the nearest port to Harlech. Small ships carried coal, building materials and lime, and there were several ship-building yards here too.

As the road ends, bear right, immediately before a house called '**Llechollwyn**'. Pick your way along the bottom of the rocks and then bear left along the edge of the saltmarsh.

2. At low tide you can walk along the very edge of the marsh beside the sands of **Afon Dwyryd,** as this is the easiest and most pleasant route. But if the tide is high or turning, keep to the left, at the upper edge of the marsh, below the rocks.

The views here are stunning, and there are several benches situated near the rocks that take full advantage of their glorious position. Look to the left and you'll see the wide sands of the Dwyryd Estuary stretching out to meet the Irish Sea in Tremadoc Bay. Half left are the settlements of Borth-y-Gest and Porthmadog, sitting prettily below the flat-topped hill of Moel-y-Gest. The sands between here and there are called Traeth Bach, literally meaning 'Small Sands'. Straight ahead is the Italianate village of Portmeirion, and to the

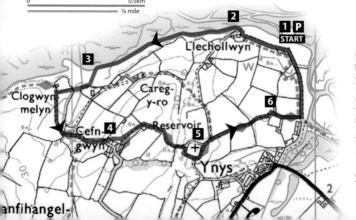

Tidal edge: *Walking along the edge of the saltmarshes*

far right is the Vale of Ffestiniog, flanked by the Moelwyns on the northern side of the valley and the foothills of the Rhinogs on the south side.

3. After about half a mile, you'll see a **large house** on the left, with cottages on either side (over to the right and left). If you've walked along the edge of the marshes, turn inland now to aim for the house. When you reach it, bear right to follow a low stone wall immediately in front, then cross a stream.

Continue ahead to cross a stile over a wall near a gate at **Clogwyn Melyn Farm** and walk ahead to meet the farm track. Turn left along the track and follow it to a junction signed for the **Wales Coast Path**. Bear right uphill to a gate before a farm.

4. Go through the gate then immediately turn left up to a kissing gate. Go through the gate into a field and bear right towards a telegraph pole with a waymarker on it. The right of way now follows the wall on the right. At the corner of the wall (and another waymarker) turn right and carry on to

Shifting sands: *Looking across Traeth Bach towards Porthmadog and Portmeirion*

another corner. Turn right here, but soon turn left, away from the wall, and follow the path down to a gate.

Go through the gate and walk down the steps and up the other side. Turn right to walk alongside the church wall. Follow it to the front of **Llanfihangel-y-Traethau Church** and turn left through the church gate to explore.

The church's circular enclosure is a clue to its antiquity. Outside the west door is a carved stone, erected sometime in the 12th century. Its Latin inscription translates as:

'Here is the the grave of Wledr, mother of Hoedliw, who first built this church in the time of King Owain Gwynedd'. *By the Middle Ages, the church was a rendezvous for pilgrims waiting to make the perilous, two-mile crossing of the Dwyryd and Glaslyn estuaries on their way to Bardsey.*

5. Leave the church and turn left through a kissing gate. At first, walk beside the church wall; but then veer right, away from the wall under overhead cables. Aim for a waymarker by a wall and a gate. Don't go through the gate, instead bear right, keeping the wall on your left, and walk down to the small gate in the corner of the field.

Go through the gate and continue straight ahead through the field. Go through another gate (or over the stile) in the corner and keep ahead, now with the low wall on your right.

6. At the end of this field, go through a gate and into a walled track. Follow this to a gate and road. Go through the gate and turn left to return to the car park to complete the walk. ♦

Llanfihangel-y-Traethau Church
This pretty medieval church was originally built on a rocky, tidal outcrop. The name means 'St Michael's on the Shores'. Interestingly, there are several shore-side churches dedicated to St Michael along Britain's Celtic coast; probably the best known is St Michael's Mount, in Cornwall. The connection with the sea here is strong; look out for the fascinating inscriptions on the many old seamen's graves in the churchyard.

Leaving the shelter of the dunes at Harlech for the open beach

Harlech Beach & Llanfair Cliffs

A moderate walk with stunning views, a stretch of beach and a historic castle and town

What to expect:
Farmland paths, quiet lanes, beach and town roads

Distance/time: 7km / 4½ miles. Allow 2–2½ hours

Start: Bron-y-Graig Uchaf long stay Pay & Display car park in the centre of Harlech. Short stay is next to the road, long stay around the corner

Grid ref: SH 582 309

Ordnance Survey Map: OS Explorer OL 18 Snowdonia *Harlech, Porthmadog & Y Bala*

After the walk: Cafés, restaurants and pubs in Harlech

Walk outline

Climbing to the lush farmland above the town of Harlech gives tremendous views across the Bay. On a clear day you can see the long arm of the Llŷn Peninsula reaching out into the wide Irish Sea. The walk then drops down through the quiet village of Llanfair, before snaking down steep steps near the cliffs to join the beach for almost a mile. The walk finally returns up a steep hill to Harlech Castle and the town.

Harlech

Harlech is a quiet town dominated by the dark and brooding castle that sits handsomely on its rock, keeping watch over Tremadog Bay. It is one of Edward I's iron ring of castles, built along the coast of Wales in the twelfth century to subdue the Welsh. Harlech is one of Edward's most imposing castles.

Many of Harlech's visitors come for the wide sandy beach and historic castle, but there are hidden gems to be found on the rolling hills behind the town. These gentle pastures give some of the best views in the area—where the magnificent sweep of Tremadog Bay merges into the sea-blue distance.

Castle from the dunes

Pyramidal orchid

Harlech strand: *It's easy to find your own space on one of the largest beaches in Wales*

The Walk

1. Leave the car park and turn right along the road. At the next junction, turn left, uphill.

At the end of the road by metal posts go straight up and then very soon bear left for a signed grassy path. At the top of the path reach a rough track: turn right as waymarked (on the wall ahead) and then very soon turn left at a 'Public Footpath' sign along the road. Soon,

bear left again alongside the wall of a house to find a narrow footpath rising up ahead.

2. Follow this grassy track to some gates. Go through the first wooden gate and stay ahead for about five steps then turn left to go through a large metal gate by the waymarker on the post that points right up the grassy field.

Follow the waymarkers across the field, through gaps in two low stone walls.

It's worth pausing to turn around here and appreciate the fine and far-reaching views across the bay. If visibility is good, look for the top of Bardsey Island at the end of the Llyn Peninsula on the far left. The towns of Criccieth and Porthmadog are directly ahead with Snowdon sitting behind them a little further to the right. The Moelwyns and Cnicht are the mountains on the far right.

Continue ahead to a stile in a stone wall. Cross it and follow the obvious path through the field to a gap in another stone wall. Go through the gap and continue with the wall to your right. At the top of the field, bear right through another gap and then left to join a **green lane** flanked by walls.

At the end of the lane is an open field. Turn right and follow the stone wall beneath power lines. As the wall veers right, ignore a gap but stay ahead to aim for some houses and eventually reach a stile over the wall.

Don't cross this stile, but instead turn left and walk alongside the wall to reach a gate onto a lane.

3. Turn right along the lane and then, almost immediately, bear left at a 'Public Footpath' sign by a **cattle grid**. Over the grid, bear immediately right onto a grassy path leading to a small gate into a field.

Bear right, to cross the field diagonally, passing some stone piles and an

electricity pole on the left, heading towards the field corner then look right for a stone stile over the wall.

Cross it and head straight down this field through a gateway and onto a

0   1km
½ mile

Sea View: *Harlech beach stretches away into the distance from the top of Harlech Cliff*

grassy track. Continue ahead again down the field, staying quite close to the wall on the right and you'll soon see a wall beginning on the left. There's a path (sometimes overgrown and muddy) between these two walls so follow this straight down to a gate onto a lane.

4. At the lane turn right, then at the crossroads go straight over, passing a bus stop. At the next junction, turn right along the pavement until you see a coast path waymarker and **National Trust sign** opposite.

5. Cross the road and go through the gate then follow the path down **Harlech Cliffs** as it zig-zags to some steps to the **railway line**. Cross the line, go down to the beach and turn right.

6. Walk along **Harlech beach** for just over a mile to reach a red and white pole and lifebelt at the main entrance. Turn right here to follow the sandy path to a tarmac track. Go through the gate and pass a **car park** on the left.

Continue ahead along the lane past the school and at the end turn right. Cross the railway line then very soon cross the road and bear left for a lane signposted for the 'Town Centre'.

7. Follow this as it zig-zags steeply uphill, eventually passing **Harlech Castle** on the left. Continue, to reach a junction with the **High Street** and turn right.

Walk along the High Street, then after a pretty cobbled square turn left up a steep footpath which leads past **St Tanwg's Church** and back to the car park to complete the walk. ♦

Harlech Castle
Harlech is one of Edward I's finest Welsh castles. It took a thousand men seven years to build and was completed in 1290. It was attacked almost immediately by Welsh freedom fighters. Captured by Owain Glyndwr in the fifteenth century, it became his home and headquarters for four years before being retaken by the English Prince Henry. Today, Harlech Castle is a designated UNESCO World Heritage Site cared for by Cadw.

Yachts in the harbour at Shell Island

Shell Island

An easy walk that explores impressive sand dunes and a wide sandy beach

Distance/time: 10km / 6 miles. Allow 3–3½ hours

Start: River Artro Car Park. From Llanbedr, follow the signs for Shell Island. The car park is ½ mile down the minor road

Grid ref: SH 581 269

Ordnance Survey Map: OS Explorer OL 18 Snowdonia: *Harlech, Porthmadog & Y Bala*

After the walk: Cafés on Shell Island (seasonal only) or the Victoria Inn at Llanbedr

Walk outline

This varied walk begins with a riverside amble before heading towards the coast to explore some of the finest sand dunes on the Cardigan Bay coastline, as well as a vast campsite and a pretty beach. The return journey is made alongside an old airfield before returning to the car park by a quiet lane.

Shell Island

Shell Island is actually a small, rounded peninsula lying just south of Harlech. The causeway to it floods at high tide, creating a sandy island characterised by marshland and dunes. The 'island' was created in the early 19th century when the Earl of Winchelsey diverted the River Artro to create a better wharf at nearby Pensarn, from where slate cargoes from Llanbedr and Llanfair were shipped.

Shell Island sign

Shell Island has been popular with campers since the 1960s. At 300 acres, it's one of the largest campsites in Europe; and its coastal location within the Snowdonia National Park and rugged layout on rolling dunes make it immensely popular throughout the summer months.

Collecting shells

The Walk

1. Take the footpath in the right hand corner of the car park. Follow the path alongside **Afon Artro**, keeping the water on your right.

The tiny River Artro starts its journey just five miles to the east at Llyn Cwm Bychan, near the Roman Steps. The River Cwmnantcol joins it at Pentre Gwynfryn, and together they head west to spill out into the estuary.

Don't cross the river but keep ahead along the bank. Cross the railway line, go through the gate and continue along the riverside path, passing **Pensarn harbour** on the right. Cross a stile and continue along the track to a tarmac road.

This is the **causeway to Shell Island**, which is covered and

impassable at high tide. A notice board shows safe crossing times.

2. Bear right, then left to follow the causeway onto **Mochras, or Shell Island**. Just before the entrance to the campsite at a large 'Welcome' sign, turn left onto a minor path. Though faint at times, it follows the high tide line with marsh to the left and dunes to the right. Continue around a low headland past a warning sign.

Shortly, head up a low hill to a lane, go straight across and down a stony track. At a junction with a tarmac road with high dunes ahead, turn right and continue to the crossroads. Turn left

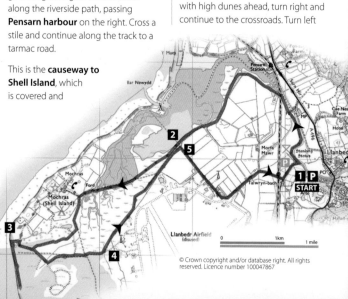

Heavenly view: Shell Island and the Artro estuary seen from the air

here, following the sign for the '**Beach Car Park'**, then turn left at the junction to enter the parking area.

Shell Island is named after the huge numbers of sea shells washed onto the beaches here during the winter. The abundance is caused by Sarn Badrig off-shore reef, which traps the shells and stops them being carried out to sea. Over 200 kinds of shell can be found; the best time to see them is between January and June.

An advert filmed here in 2010 by Visit Wales, the Welsh tourist board, was broadcast around the world.

3. It's well worth exploring the beach, saltmarsh and dunes.

Morfa Dyffryn *is a National Nature Reserve that supports some specialised plants and animals. Among a dazzling array of wildflowers, look for thrift or 'sea pinks', wild pansies, common centaury and bird's-foot trefoil. Later in the summer, the dunes are home to several rare orchids including early-marsh orchids,*

Sky mirror: *Sea-wet sand reflects the sky on Morfa Dyffryn beach*

marsh helleborines and green-flowered helleborines.

Return to the car park and retrace your route, turning right at the junction to return to the cross roads, then turn right along the road.

Follow this road through the campsite. At a T-junction keep ahead and take the next left turn down a stony track, which soon turns into a tarmac footpath.

The **Royal Aerospace Establishment** airfield here has been disused since 2004. Built in 1941 and used by the RAF throughout the Second World War, it was recently used as a weapons' training centre. It is currently owned by the Welsh Assembly Government.

4. Continue along the path, with the airfield on the right, then go through a gate onto the road.

5. Turn right along the road for about a mile to return to the car park and complete the walk

To visit the **Llanbedr,** *follow the road for another 400 metres and turn left over the stone bridge. The village grew up around the slate industry in the late 18th century.*

The tiny Welsh church of Capel Salem, in nearby Pentre Gwynfryn, is associated with the infamous 'Salem painting', by English artist Sydney Curnow Vosper. This apparently ordinary picture of a local woman was said to show the devil's face concealed in her shawl. Capel Salem is a short way up the side road next to the Victoria Inn, signposted for Cwm Bychan.♦

Sarn Badrig

At extreme low tides you may glimpse a vast glacial moraine, or shingle reef, jutting out from the beach at Shell Island. Sarn Badrig, or 'St Patrick's Causeway', is almost 12 miles long, and was once a great hazard to shipping. One casualty was 'The Diamond', whose cargo of apples washed ashore. Their pips were planted by local farmers, and today the 'Diamond' is a celebrated Welsh apple variety.

One of the two burial chambers in the Dyffryn Ardudwy Neolithic cairn

Dyffryn Ardudwy

An easy short walk to discover the secrets of two ancient burial chambers and a wild coastline

Distance/time: 5km / 3 miles. Allow 2 hours

Start: Bennar Beach Pay & Display car park . From the main A496 road near Dyffryn Ardudwy village, follow signs for Dyffryn Seaside Estate/Bennar Beach

Grid ref: SH 573 227

Ordnance Survey Map: Explorer OL 23 *Cadair Idris & Bala Lake*

After the walk: Cadwgan Hotel (halfway along the walk), café in Dyffryn Ardudwy or the Victoria Inn at Llanbedr

Walk outline

This gentle walk starts by heading away from the sea and into pretty woodland and green fields. The route then takes a small detour to the pleasant village of Dyffryn Ardudwy and up the hill behind it to the impressive site of the Neolithic burial chambers. The walk returns through the village before veering towards the coast to make the return journey along the beach.

Dyffryn Ardudwy

With the wide, unspoiled coastline of Cardigan Bay on one side and the rugged uplands of the Rhinog mountains on the other, Dyffryn Ardudwy is a pleasing village, situated between the larger towns of Harlech and Barmouth.

But the beach is probably the main draw during the long summer days—the nearby broad, golden sands stretch off into the distance, both north and south. On a clear day the sun dances across the blue waters of Cardigan Bay to glimmer on the coastal towns scattered along the far coast of the Lleyn Peninsula opposite.

National Park sign

Lapwing

The Walk

1. With your back to the sea, leave the parking area and walk back along the road you drove down, for around half a mile.

Just after the large house on the right, called **Bennar Fawr**, look for a footpath sign on the left. Go through the gate and follow the path towards the trees.

Cross the footbridge over the stream, go through another gate and over a second bridge. Continue through the trees and cross the **railway line**.

This is the Cambrian Line which runs between Pwllheli on the Llŷn Peninsula and Dyfi Junction, near Machynlleth. It opened in 1861 and the coastal sections of the route are regarded as one of the most scenic train journeys in Wales.

2. Go through a gate on the other side and follow the path through **Coed-y-bachau**.

At the end of the path cross a small stream and turn left onto the lane, then almost immediately right onto a signed footpath. Follow the field edge to emerge on a lane.

To visit the **Neolithic burial chambers**, or dolmens, turn right past the houses to the main road, with a shop on the corner.

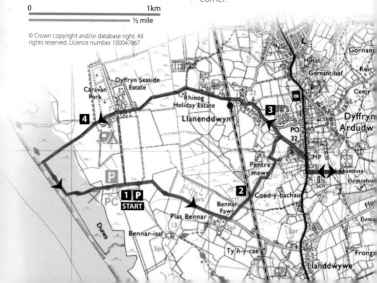

0   1km

½ mile

Beach access: *A wooden boardwalk snakes through the dunes below Dyffryn Ardudwy*

Cross the road, turn right and continue along the pavement to the brown signpost for the burial chambers. The path leads to the huge cairn with its two megalithic burial chambers.

For a short diversion, a footpath in the top right corner of the field will take you to an elegant tree-lined avenue at **Cors-y-Gedol** mansion and chapel.

This ancient manor house, whose curious name means the 'bog of hospitality', was built by the powerful local Vaughan family in the 14th century. It's said the Vaughans used their influence to put Henry VII on the throne in 1485. An older building on this spot is also reputed to have been the home of Llywelyn the Great, who once ruled much of Wales. The manor house was rebuilt in the 16th century and is now a popular wedding venue.

From the chambered tomb, retrace your steps back to the main road, turn right, and then left just before the corner shop. Now walk back along the lane, passing the stile you crossed earlier.

Sky and sea: *Light and space dominate the senses on Morfa Dyffryn's vast, open beach*

3. At the next junction, turn left and follow the winding road past houses and over a level crossing. Nearby is the **Cadwgan Hotel**.

Continue along the road as it becomes a stony track and bear left at a footpath sign. Follow the path through a gate into a holiday park. Walk along the tarmac road and keep straight ahead at a mini roundabout.

Continue past the campsite shop and restaurant, and through a gate. Bear right here, and follow the waymarker

arrows through a second gate onto the long path leading to the sand dunes. A final gate takes you into the dunes.

The extensive dunes here are part of the **Morfa Dyffryn National Nature Reserve** *and home to a rich variety of butterflies, insects and wildflowers, including orchids, rare fungi and lichens. This precious habitat also supports several declining species of birds including skylarks, lapwings and choughs.*

4. Walk straight through the dunes, drop down to the beach, and turn left.

Sections of this beach are an official **naturist beach***; in the summer, signs mark the designated areas. It has been*

popular with naturists since at least the 1930s, and is widely regarded as one of the best places for being naked in Britain.

Continue along the beach until you reach a tall red and white pole. Turn left here and follow the boardwalk through the dunes to the road. Follow the road past a sculpture and back to the car park to complete the walk. ♦

Neolithic chambered cairn

Built around 6,000 years ago, the Dyffryn Ardudwy burial chambers are the best of a group of portal dolmens on these west-facing coastal slopes. Excavation in the 1960s showed the two well-preserved burial chambers were constructed at different times and were originally covered with a cairn of stones. Much like a parish church, the monument once stood at the heart of a small prehistoric farming community.

Barmouth harbour

Barmouth & Arthog

A moderate walk that crosses Barmouth's iconic bridge then explores the pretty woodland across the estuary

What to expect:
Well-marked footpaths, woodland paths and quiet lanes

Distance/time: 10km / 6 miles. Allow 3½–4 hours

Start: Barmouth's main Pay & Display car park on the sea-front. Toll charges apply for pedestrians crossing the bridge

Grid ref: SH 613 155

Ordnance Survey Map: OS Explorer OL 23 Snowdonia: *Cadair Idris & Bala Lake*

After the walk: Cafés, restaurants and pubs in Barmouth

Walk outline
From the bustling resort of Barmouth this walk crosses the famous bridge from where you can stop and admire stunning views both out towards the coast and along the Mawddach Estuary. The route follows the estuary eastwards before heading inland and climbing a pretty forest path alongside the Arthog Waterfalls. It descends along quiet country lanes and back towards the sea to join the Mawddach Trail. The return is back over the bridge to appreciate those views again!

Barmouth
From humble beginnings as a small port exporting woven cloth, slate and copper to the Americas, **Barmouth** became a fashionable holiday hotspot for people from the crowded English cities soon after new railway links first made the fresh air and restorative sea breezes accessible.

When the railway arrived in 1867, it brought not only industry and jobs but also tourists—with money to spend. Barmouth soon grew to become one of Cardigan Bay's most popular resorts. This lovely walk explores both the hustle of the town and the tranquility of the woods and waterfalls across the estuary.

CYNGOR GWY_
PONT DOLL ABERMAW
TALIADAU:-

OEDOLION	90c
PLANT (O DAN 16)	50c
WYTHNOSOL (OEDOLION)	£3.00
WYTHNOSOL (PLANT)	£1.50
TOCYNNAU BLYNYDDOL OEDOLION	£20.00
TOCYNNAU BLYNYDDOL PLANT	£10.00
OEDOLION A BEICIAU	£1.50
PLANT A BEICIAU	£1.00
BEICIAU MODUR AC OEDOLION	£2.50

Bridge tolls

Cuckoo

The Walk

1. Face the beach and turn left along the road. Walk round the corner past the **harbour master's office** and **yacht club**. Go under the railway bridge, turn right past the **Last Inn**, and continue along the pavement. Beyond the rocks, a path leads down to the bridge on the right. There is a fee for pedestrians.

2. Cross **Barmouth Bridge**.

It's worth stopping halfway across to admire the view. If you look to the left you will see the wide mouth of the Mawddach Estuary stretching into the distance,

framed by the foothills of Cadair Idris on the right and the Rhinogs on the far left. There is a cycle track along the estuary (the Mawddach Trail) that leads to Dolgellau, following the route of an old railway line.

At the end of the bridge, go left over a stile and follow the line of a rocky embankment, aiming for the lefthand edge of the wooded hill of **Fegla Fawr**, ahead. Follow the grassy path around its northern flank.

3. At the terrace of houses overlooking the estuary, follow the signed public footpath around the back.

Mawddach Crescent was built in the early 1900s by entrepreneur Solomon Andrews. His intention was to build a complete holiday resort here, but most of the land proved to be unusable. During the Second World War the terrace was taken over by the Royal Marines as a training centre.

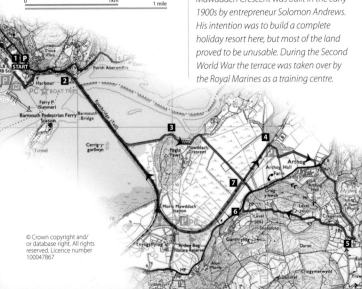

Bridge over troubled waters: *Barmouth's iconic bridge over the Mawddach Estuary*

At the tarmac lane turn left, then almost immediately right along a rough path. Just before you reach the cattle grid at the drive for **Bryn Celyn**, turn right and go through the gate. Go immediately through another gate straight ahead (ignore the gate to the left) and along the path across marshy land.

These boggy fields form part of the **Arthog Bog Nature Reserve**: *a small wetland with a wealth of wildlife, from cuckoos and warblers to rare butterflies.*

Follow the path and go through the gates to reach an old railway embankment, now the **Mawddach Trail**. Turn left.

4. Follow the Trail to the next gate. Beyond the gate, turn right onto a tarmac lane, and then climb over a signed ladder stile on the left. Bear right along the grassy embankment. Cross another stile and follow the path to **Saint Catherine's Church**.

Go through the gate onto the main road. Turn left and almost immediately right to find a signed footpath heading

Wood and iron: *Walkers cross the Mawddach Estuary beside the train tracks*

up steps; follow this uphill and through the trees.

At the top of the first climb, keep ahead and follow the waymarkers to a right turn. Continue on the winding path uphill through the trees, alongside waterfalls.

Eventually you'll reach a ladder stile by a large tree. Continue over two ladder stiles. At the final stile with an old slate bridge ahead, turn right for a grassy track and gate.

To the left here, over the hills, lie the Cregennen Lakes: two beautiful natural pools in the shadow of Cadair Idris.

5. Go through the gate to a lane and turn right. Follow the lane downhill to a fork with a stony track signposted as a bridleway. Turn left through the gate towards 'Ty'n y Graig and Merddyn',

Walk past **Merddyn cottage** downhill through the woods. At a gate on the right, stay left. Towards the bottom of the woods, go through two wooden gates and down a track to a lane. Turn right, and right again at the main road.

6. Walk briefly along the pavement, then

turn left across the road, and take the signed path to the **Mawddach Trail**.

7. Turn left and follow the Trail past **Morfa Mawddach** and the car park and toilets, to the foot of the bridge.

Cross over **Barmouth Bridge** once more and retrace your steps to the car park to complete the walk. ♦

Barmouth Bridge

Opened in 1897, Barmouth's iconic bridge greeted 19th-century tourists as they flocked to the new resort. Today, the bridge is as much a part of the town as its seaside rock and donkey rides. At 2,300 feet long, it's the longest viaduct in Wales and Britain's longest wooden railway bridge. Strong currents in the estuary meant that each iron support had to be sunk 120 feet into the sea bed, and two workmen drowned during its construction.

Cadair Idris and Afon Mawddach

Barmouth Panorama

A classic short walk with the most spectacular views in Barmouth

What to expect:
Quiet lanes, well-marked paths and the famous Panorama Gardens

Distance/time: 6km / 3½ miles. Allow 2–2½ hours

Start: Panorama car park (leave the A496 Dolgellau Road at the eastern end of Porkington Terrace for Panorama Road. Follow this to the Snowdonia National Park Car Park

Grid ref: SH 625 166

Ordnance Survey Map: OS Explorer OL 23 Snowdonia: *Cadair Idris & Bala Lake*

After the walk: Cafés, restaurants and pubs in Barmouth

Walk outline

The Panorama Walk is one of Barmouth's classic circuits, and once you reach the Gardens it's easy to see why. The walk begins from the Panorama car park above Barmouth. It then follows a quiet farm lane, explores pretty woodland and a historic village before tracing an old drover's road to the Panorama Gardens.

Barmouth

The arrival of the railway in the mid-1800s transformed Barmouth from a small village to a fashionable holiday destination. Health-mad Victorian society was attracted here by the fresh coastal breezes and sea bathing.

National Park sign

Celebrities and artists of the time such as Ruskin, Shelley, Darwin, Turner and Tennyson flocked to Barmouth. Even Wordsworth was tempted away from his beloved Lake District. In fact, he described the panorama over the Mawddach as 'sublime', and this walk certainly shows off the best of Barmouth's views.

The views are at their best on a sunny day when the sweep of the estuary is breathtaking.

Red kite

The Walk

1. Leave the car park and continue along the lane ahead, past a 'No Through Road' sign.

Follow the lane for just over a mile, then go through a gate and cross a small stream. Soon afterwards, where the road kinks sharply to the left, pass through a gate on the right and go down a stony track towards a barn. Follow the

waymarked path behind the barn and continue through a gate into a field.

Bear right across the field, keeping close to a wall on the right, and walk downhill through a wooden gate. Then follow the winding path through the woods.

2. At a waymarker opposite a stone stile, turn right and follow this path over three further stiles. Beyond the third one, the woodland opens out close to a junction of paths. Turn left here and head downhill alongside the wall.

Follow this path past a house and chapel, then keep ahead, downhill, on the lane.

*You have just walked through the tiny hamlet of **Cutiau** (literally meaning 'sties' or 'huts'). The chapel is now a private house, but it was once a Congregationalist Chapel built in 1806.*

3. As the lane bends sharp left (with some iron gates ahead) turn right to follow a narrow track between two walls.

At a path junction and 'Public Footpath' signs, bear right, uphill, past crumbling ruins below.

*These are the remains of **Bwlch-y-Goedleoedd**, thought to be an old inn. The famous Welsh poet Dafydd ap*

0   1km

½ mile

Inn ruins?: *All that remains of an old drovers' inn on the pass above Barmouth*

Gwilym reputedly stayed here. Born around 1315, he is widely regarded as one of the greatest poets in Welsh history.

4. Eventually you'll reach a gate on the left signposted for the **Panorama Walk**. Follow the obvious path (enjoying breathtaking views along the way) and complete the circuit back to the gate.

In Wordsworth's day entry to the panorama, its tearoom and gardens cost one penny, but today admission is free!

Pass through the gate, turn left, and go through two further gates to a lane. Now turn right to reach the car park and complete the walk. ♦

The Mawddach Estuary

The river Mawddach begins high in the Arenig Hills, some 20 miles north-east of Barmouth. By the time it reaches its wide, sandy mouth near Dolgellau it is in full flow. The estuary is renowned for its natural beauty and is well worth exploring. Along its southern bank runs the Mawddach Trail, a path and cycleway that follows the railway line that ran between Barmouth and Ruabon until the 'Beeching Cuts' of the 1960s.

Aberdyfi

Aberdyfi

A pleasant stroll above the pretty town of Aberdyfi, with stunning estuary views

What to expect:
Well-marked public footpaths, farmland tracks (vague in places), quiet lanes and beach

Distance/time: 5.5km / 3½ miles. Allow 2 hours

Start: Pay and Display car park by the Tourist Information Centre in the middle of Aberdyfi

Grid ref: SN 614 959

Ordnance Survey Map: OS Explorer OL 23 Snowdonia: *Cadair Idris & Bala Lake*

After the walk: Cafés and restaurants in Aberdyfi

Walk outline

This walk starts in the pretty coastal village of Aberdyfi before heading up into the rolling hills and farmland above. There are sensational views across the Dyfi Estuary and northwards along the Cardigan Bay coastline. The route crosses the top of one small valley before heading down another and dropping to sea level. The walk back to the village centre is made along the beach.

Aberdyfi

Sitting prettily on the banks of the Dyfi estuary, the village of Aberdyfi grew up around the ship building and fishing industries. Because of its strategic location in the centre of Wales, it has always been a popular destination. It's thought the Romans built a road into Aberdyfi around AD80, but it was the 19th-century industrial revolution that turned this sleepy fishing village into one of the busiest ports on the coast, exporting mainly slate and oak.

Today, Aberdyfi is a popular tourist destination thanks to its stunning coastal location, sandy beaches and traditional activities like donkey rides, bowling and fishing.

Donkey rides

Atlantic grey seal

The Walk

1. With your back to the **Tourist Information Centre** and the beach, turn right along the main street, then almost immediately left up **Copperhill Street**. Walk under the railway bridge.

Very soon, look for a signposted public footpath on the left and follow it uphill past two houses called **Bryniau Isaf**. Turn sharp right here and walk uphill to some steps. Continue until the path becomes a wider track.

Follow this to a tarmac road and continue to a junction. Cross the road here to a wooden gate marked by a public footpath sign.

2. Go through the gate and turn left, behind a house. The path winds alongside a fence before eventually climbing steeply uphill to a stile.

Continue ahead over another stile and keep straight on, passing a bench on your right. Walk through a field, keeping the fence on your left. The path narrows, with a gorse covered hill to the right.

3. The path eventually drops to a small stream by a footpath sign and gate. Cross the stream, go through the gate and turn left, then bear slightly right, around the rear of the house towards a metal gate with a waymarker.

Go through the gate, down the hill and turn right at the public footpath sign to walk behind the caravans. At the last caravan, bear right to a stile.

Cross the stile and keep ahead across the undulating field. The path is vague in places here, but stay roughly ahead, bearing ever so slightly left. Around 400 metres later the derelict buildings of **Trefeddian Fach farm** should appear in front of you; if you end up either

Sand and sea: *Aberdyfi enjoys both stunning beaches and the clear waters of Cardigan Bay*

above or below them, just walk towards the buildings to correct your course. Walk in front of the buildings, then head between two low summits to a track.

4. Turn left, and follow the steep road downhill. Eventually, you'll reach a gate opposite a **cemetery**; go through and turn left towards the main road. Cross the road to a parking area and find a track heading downhill on the left. Follow this to the railway, cross carefully and continue on the track over the **golf course**. It leads to a boardwalk onto the beach.

5. Turn left along the beach back to **Aberdyfi** to complete the walk. ♦

Dyfi Bells

Aberdyfi is the setting for the historic folk song The Bells of Aberdovey, *written by the 18th-century English composer Charles Dibdin. The song tells how the church bells still ring in the legendary kingdom of Cantre'r Gwaelod, deep beneath the waters of Cardigan Bay. In honour of the poem, an enormous bronze bell was installed at Aberdyfi Pier in 2011. Just as it does in the poem, the bell tolls as the tide rises.*

On the coast path below the war memorial

Borth & Wallog

A rugged circular walk starting on the stunning Ceredigion Coast Path and returning inland over pleasant farmland

What to expect:
Waymarked undulating coast path, quiet lanes and farmland

Distance/time: 10km / 6½ miles. Allow 4 hours

Start: Close to the RNLI lifeboat station at the southern end of Borth, near the roundabout. Park on the roadside or at the village car park a little further north

Grid ref: SN 607 889

Ordnance Survey Map: OS Explorer 213 *Aberystwyth & Cwm Rheidol*

After the walk: Cafés and restaurants in Borth or Machynlleth

Walk outline
The first section of this walk follows the Ceredigion Coast Path southwards, offering spectacular coastal views across Cardigan Bay and down to the steep grey cliffs and the sparkling sea below. The path rises and falls several times as it follows every undulation of the coast, before heading inland to return through pretty farmland and quiet country lanes.

The Ceredigion Coast Path
The Ceredigion Coast Path stretches for sixty miles between Ynys Las, north of Aberystwyth, to the town of Cardigan in the south. This beautiful coastline offers fabulous views: on a clear day they stretch as far south as Fishguard and north to the craggy arm of the Llŷn Peninsula. The path is rugged and skirts the top of cliffs in places, so care is needed.

Cilfftop war memorial

This part of Cardigan Bay has one of the largest populations of bottlenose dolphins in Europe, with as many as 200 over-summering here. You may also be lucky enough to spot porpoise, seals, basking sharks and even the occasional leatherback turtle.

Bottlenose dolphins

The Walk

1. With the sea on your right, walk south along the road (bearing right at the roundabout if you've parked further up in the village). Head for the **memorial** on the hill above the cliffs. Turn right into **Cliff Road**.

Walk past the houses on the left and, at the end of the road, bear right to follow a footpath sign for the Wales Coast Path. Follow the path uphill, through a gate and on towards the **war memorial**.

Stop to catch your breath here and enjoy the stunning views north and south, and to the village of Borth below. Borth (which means 'The Port') is popular with tourists during the summer thanks to its long sandy beaches. The Ynyslas Sand Dunes begin at the

northern end of the village, and are part of a nature reserve that attracts a good variety of wildlife and birds.

Above the ocean: *The Wales Coast Path hugs the clifftop south of Borth*

The coast path now continues ahead, following the fence line. Take care as you walk along the path—it can be close to the edge at times. Follow as it undulates for over a mile, until you eventually reach the inlet at **Wallog**, where you'll see a large house and scattered buildings on the far side.

Wallog is an isolated inlet with a single house and a collection of farm buildings. There's an old but well preserved lime kiln at the end of the bay which was used to process the limestone that was shipped here and then spread over the farmland of Wallog estate. At low tide it's sometimes possible to spot the stony shingle spit of Sarn Gynfelyn that starts here and juts out from the beach.

2. Cross the bottom of the hilly field towards the house then go over the stream at a **stone footbridge**. To explore the beach and **lime kiln**, turn right here and then retrace your steps afterwards. Otherwise, turn left up the drive to go through the gate and

Spectacular bay: *The cliff path at Borth gives spectacular views of the northern half of Cardigan Bay*

follow the track uphill, passing the farm buildings on the left.

Keep ahead to eventually pass another farm and then a drive on the left. When you reach the road, turn left uphill; around 500 metres later, take the first turning on the right into a narrow lane.

3. The lane runs through the fields. Roughly a mile later, look for a signposted bridleway on the left. Turn down the lane and continue to the farm. At the corner of the first barn, turn right and go through a small gate into a hilly field. Walk uphill to another gate in the top lefthand corner of the field.

4. Go through the gate and turn right up a short, steep track. At the top you'll come to a junction of gates; go through the one on the right (look for the blue bridleway sign on the gatepost) and walk along the edge of the field with the hedge on your left.

At the top of the field are two gates; go through the lefthand one. Keep straight ahead, to cross the edge of the field. Go through another gate, cross the field to two wooden gates and go through them.

5. Turn right along the lane. Roughly 100 metres later, turn left into another lane. Follow this for around 700 metres to a cross roads and turn left again.

Follow this winding road downhill, eventually passing a **caravan park** before coming to a junction.

6. Turn right and head downhill to return to the **lifeboat station** to complete the walk. ♦

Fossilised forest

At low tide the retreating seawater reveals the haunting sight of an ancient submerged forest. Stumps, twigs and branches of old oak, willow and birch trees are half buried in the sand. The forest dates from around 3,500BC: proof that the land once reached much further out. According to local legend, the forest is all that remains of an ancient kingdom called Cantre'r Gwaelod, or the 'Lowland Hundred'.

Useful Information

Wales Coast Path

Comprehensive information about all sections of the Wales Coast Path can be found at: **www.walescoastpath.co.uk**

Visit Wales

The Visit Wales website covers everything from accommodation and events to attractions and adventure. For information on the area covered by this book, see the 'Snowdonia Mountains and Coast' section. **www.visitwales.co.uk**

Snowdonia National Park

Some of the walks in this book fall within the Snowdonia National Park. For information, maps, webcams and things to see and do, visit: **www.eryri-npa.gov.uk**

Tourist Information Centres

The main TICs provide free information on everything from accommodation and travel to what's on and walking advice.

Aberdyfi	01654 767 321	tic.aberdyfi@eryri-npa.gov.uk
Barmouth	01341 280 787	barmouth.tic@gwynedd.gov.uk
Borth	01970 871 174	borthtic@ceredigion.gov.uk
Harlech	01766 780 658	tic.harlech@eryri-npa.gov.uk
Porthmadog	01766 512 981	porthmadog.tic@gwynedd.gov.uk

Travel

Public Transport for services in all parts of Wales are detailed by Traveline Cymru. Call 0871 200 22 33 or **www.traveline-cymru.info**

Tide Times

Some of the walks in this book are dependent on tide times, and it's important to check them before starting out. For details see **www.tourism.ceredigion.gov.uk/ saesneg/tides.htm** and calculate the tide times according to location. You can also pick up Tide Tables from TICs for around £1.

Weather

The Met Office operates a 24 hour online weather forecast for Snowdonia.

Follow the link from the National Park website **www.eryri-npa.gov.uk/visiting/your-weather-forecast-service** or see **www.metoffice.gov.uk**